GRAPHIC LIBRARY

GRAPHIC HISTORY

The SALEM WITCH TRIALS

by Michael Martin

illustrated by Brian Bascle

Consultant:
Walter W. Woodward
Assistant Professor of History
University of Connecticut, Hartford

Capstone
press

Mankato, Minnesota

Graphic Library is published by Capstone Press,
151 Good Counsel Drive, P.O. Box 669, Mankato, Minnesota 56002.
www.capstonepress.com

Printed in the United States of America

1 2 3 4 5 6 10 09 08 07 06 05

Library of Congress Cataloging-in-Publication Data
Martin, Michael, 1948–
The Salem witch trials / by Michael Martin; illustrated by Brian Bascle.
p. cm.—(Graphic library. Graphic history)
Includes bibliographical references and index.
ISBN 0-7368-3847-3 (hardcover)
ISBN 0-7368-5246-8 (paperback)
1. Trials (Witchcraft)—Massachusetts—Salem—History—17th century—Juvenile literature. 2. Witchcraft—Massachusetts—Salem—Juvenile literature. I. Bascle, Brian. II. Title. III. Series.
BF1576.M36 2005
133.4'3'097445—dc22 2004019145

Summary: The story of the 1692 witchcraft trials in Salem, Massachusetts, told in graphic novel format.

Editor's note: Direct quotations from primary sources are indicated by a yellow background. Direct quotations appear on the following pages:

Pages 5, 23, from Samuel Parris' sermons, quoted in *A Delusion of Satan* by Frances Hill (New York: Doubleday, 1995).

Pages 6, 21, from Cotton Mather's *Memorable Providences, Relating to Witchcrafts and Possessions.*

Pages 8, 11, 12, 24, from *The Salem Witchcraft Papers*, edited by Paul Boyer and Stephen Nissenbaum (University of Virginia Library. http://etext.virginia.edu/salem/witchcraft/texts/transcripts.html)

Page 25, from Increase Mather's "Cases of Conscience Concerning Evil Spirits Personating Men," quoted in *Delusion of Satan* by Frances Hill (New York: Doubleday, 1995).

Page 27, from Ann Putnam's apology in 1706, quoted in *A Delusion of Satan* by Frances Hill (New York: Doubleday, 1995).

Credits

Art Director and Storyboard Artist
Jason Knudson

Art Director
Heather Kindseth

Editor
Rebecca Glaser

Acknowledgment

Capstone Press thanks Philip Charles Crawford, Library Director, Essex High School, Essex, Vermont, and columnist for *Knowledge Quest*, for his assistance in the preparation of this book.

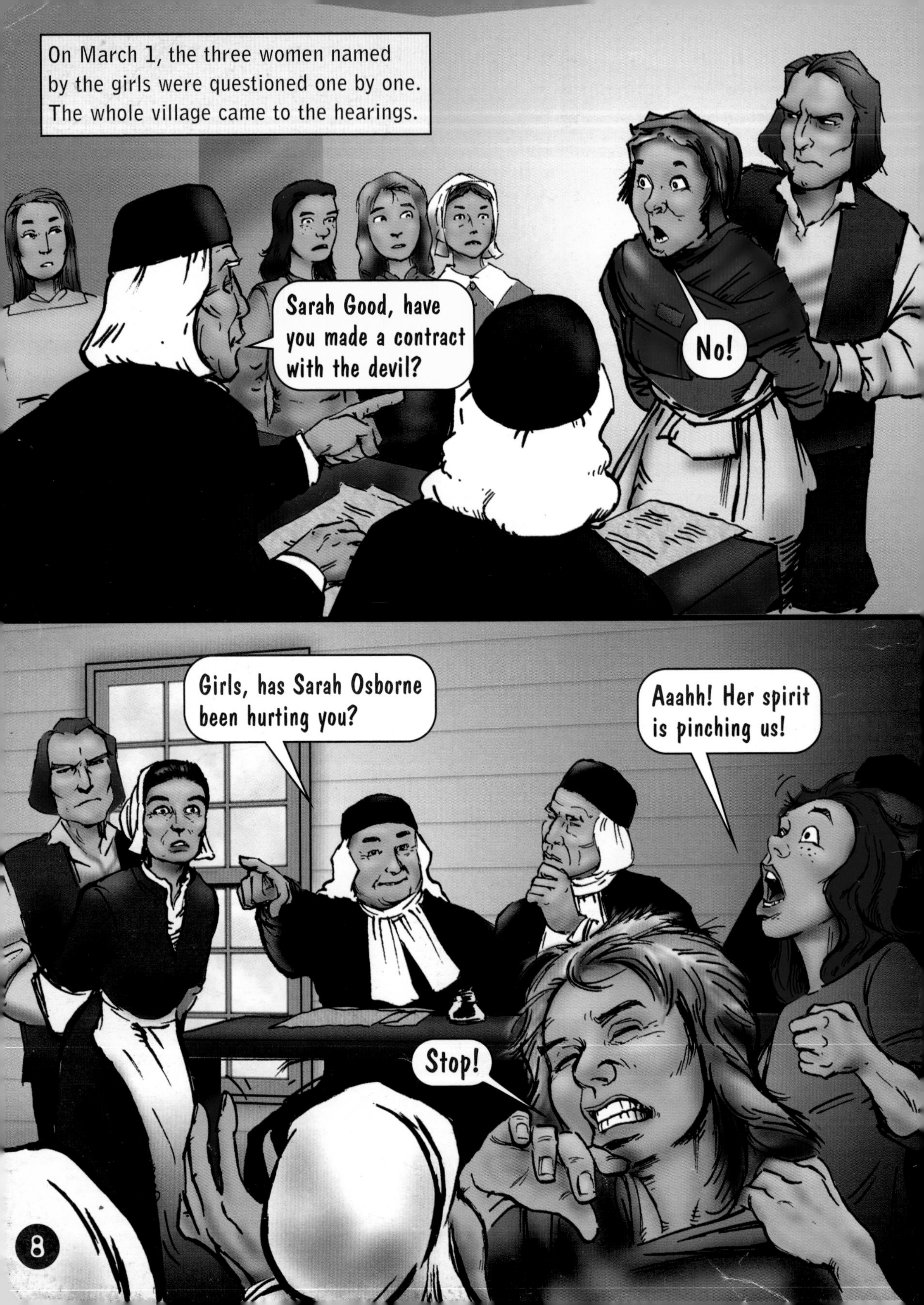
On March 1, the three women named by the girls were questioned one by one. The whole village came to the hearings.
Sarah Good, have you made a contract with the devil?
No!
Girls, has Sarah Osborne been hurting you?
Aaahh! Her spirit is pinching us!
Stop!

CHAPTER 2

More Accusations

Even though the three accused witches were in jail, the girls' fits continued.

Abigail Williams backed up Ann's claim in church the next Sunday.

What's wrong, Ann?

It's Martha Corey's spirit, Mother. She's hurting me!

Look, there on the beam. It's Martha Corey's spirit!

Villagers were shocked. No one thought that Martha Corey, a respected church member, was a witch.

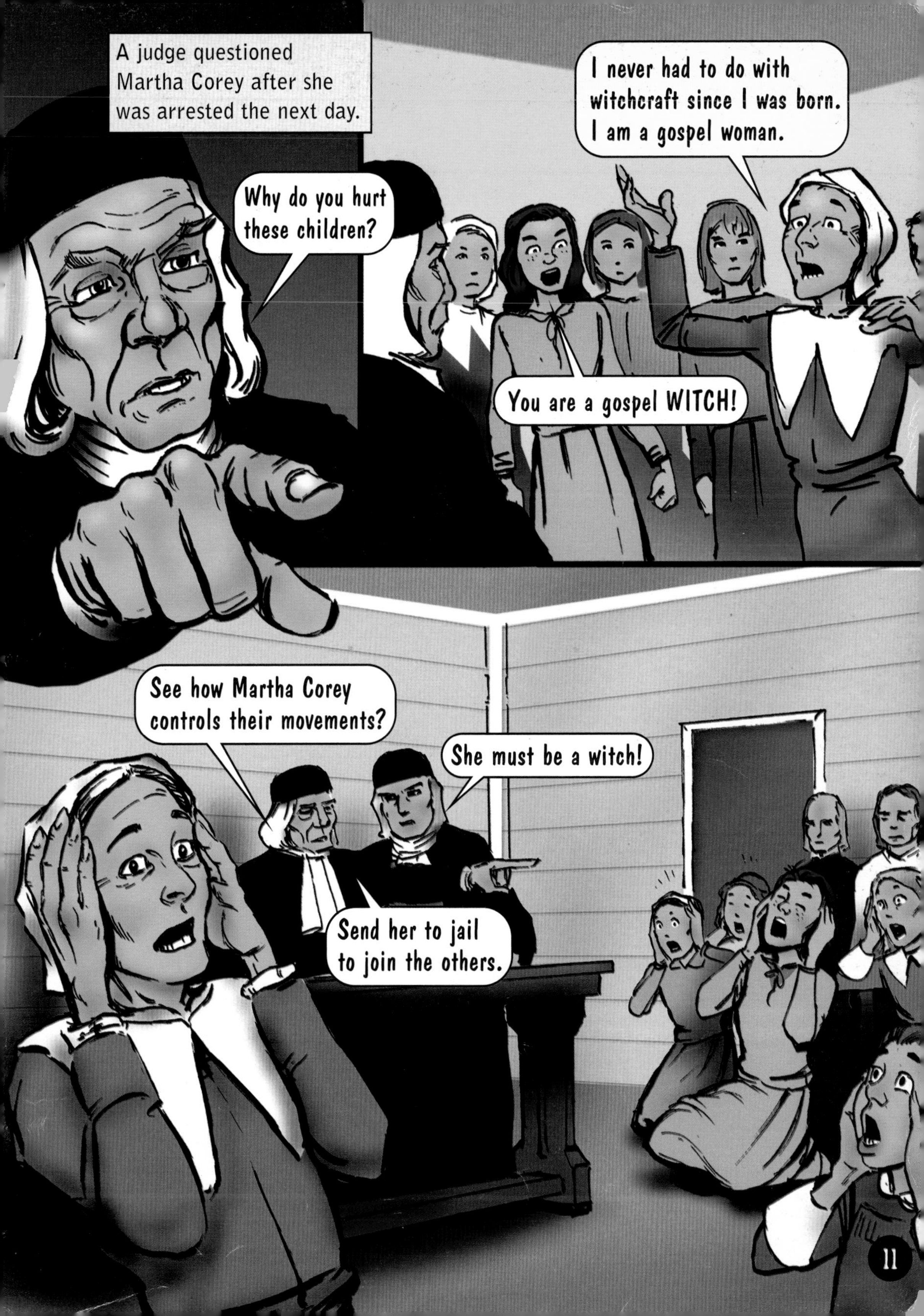
A judge questioned Martha Corey after she was arrested the next day.
Why do you hurt these children?
I never had to do with witchcraft since I was born. I am a gospel woman.
You are a gospel WITCH!
See how Martha Corey controls their movements?
She must be a witch!
Send her to jail to join the others.

After John Proctor spoke out against the girls' claims, his wife, Elizabeth, was accused of witchcraft. At the hearing, Abigail Williams gave evidence.

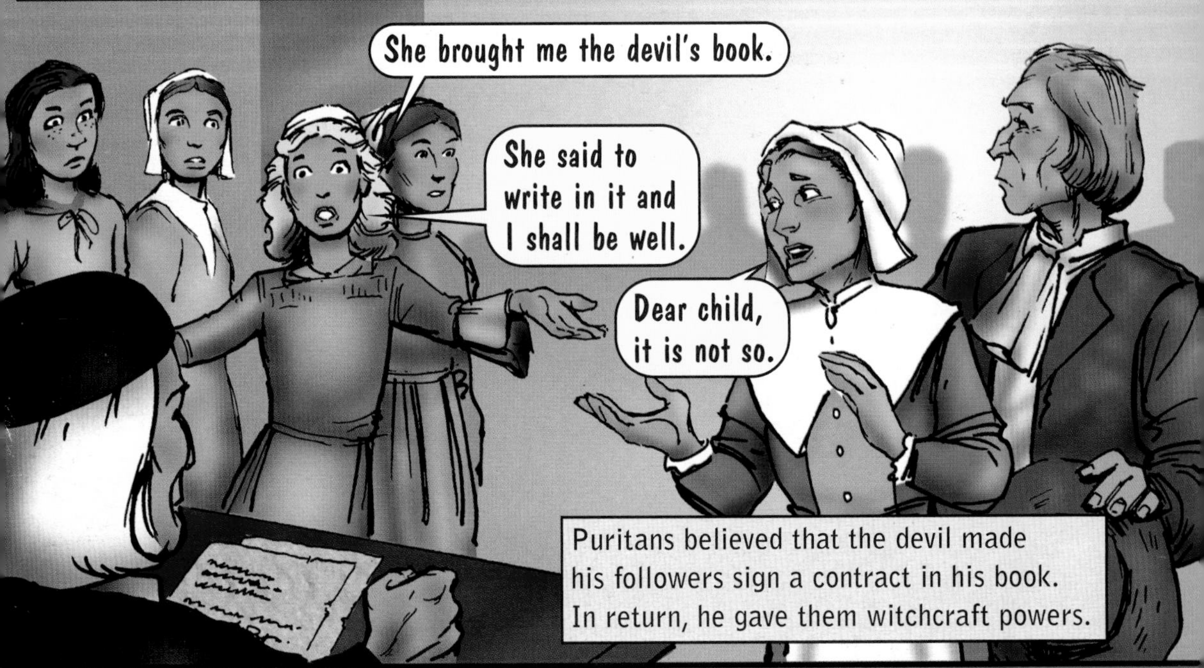
She brought me the devil's book.
She said to write in it and I shall be well.
Dear child, it is not so.

Puritans believed that the devil made his followers sign a contract in his book. In return, he gave them witchcraft powers.

Family members of the accused witches were often suspected too.

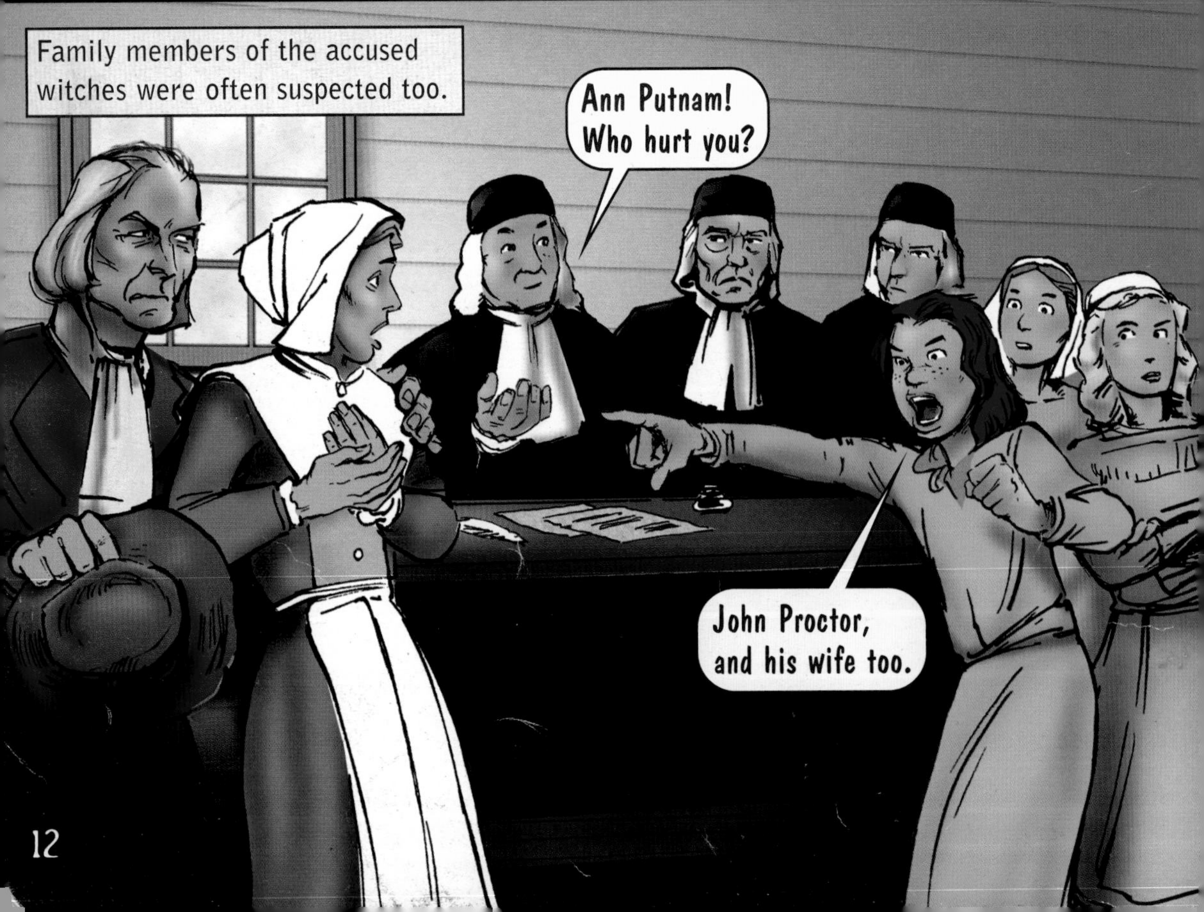
Ann Putnam! Who hurt you?
John Proctor, and his wife too.

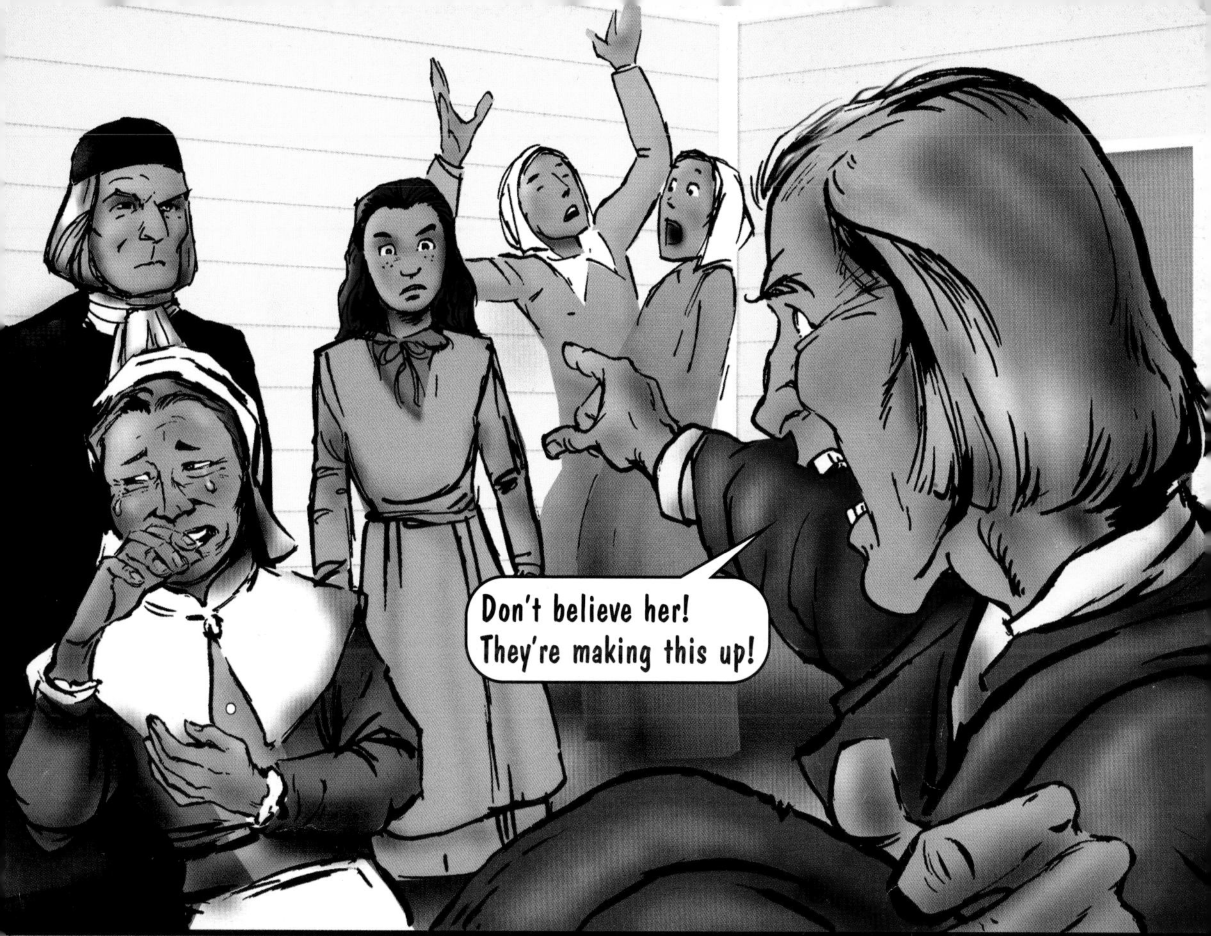
Don't believe her!
They're making this up!

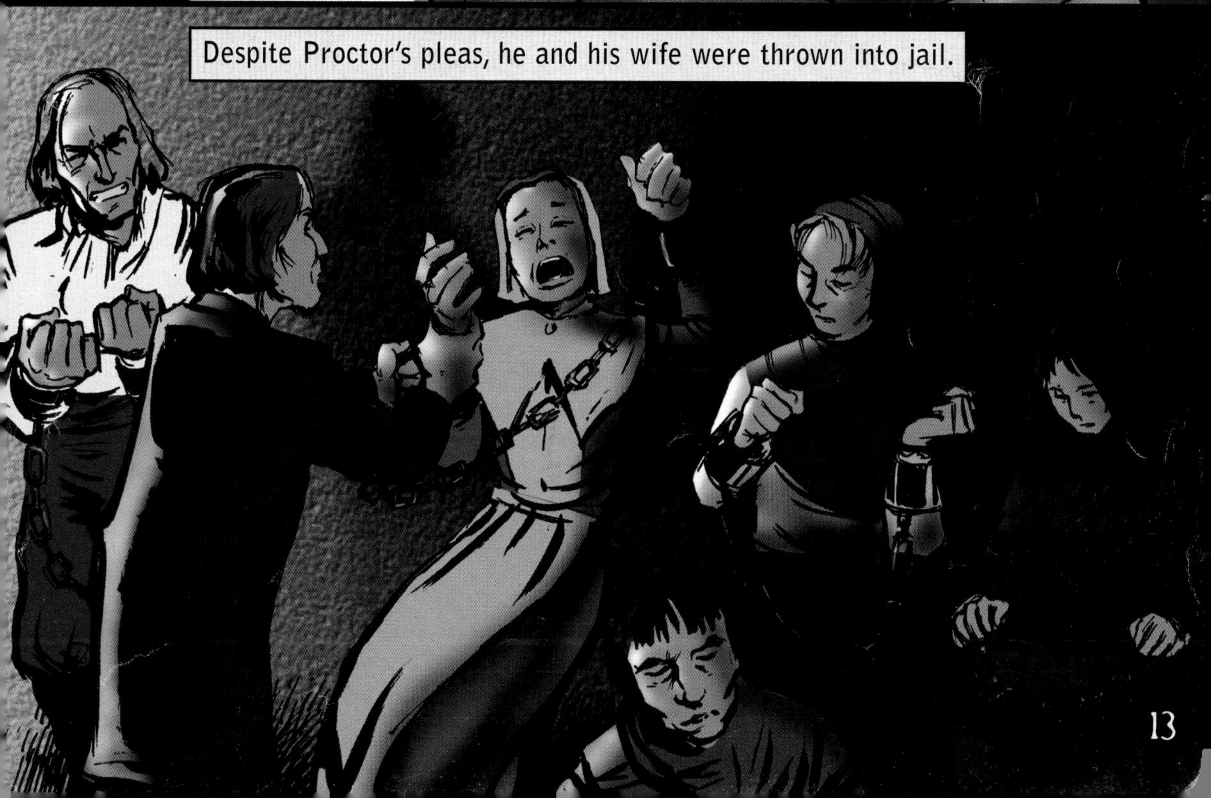
Despite Proctor's pleas, he and his wife were thrown into jail.

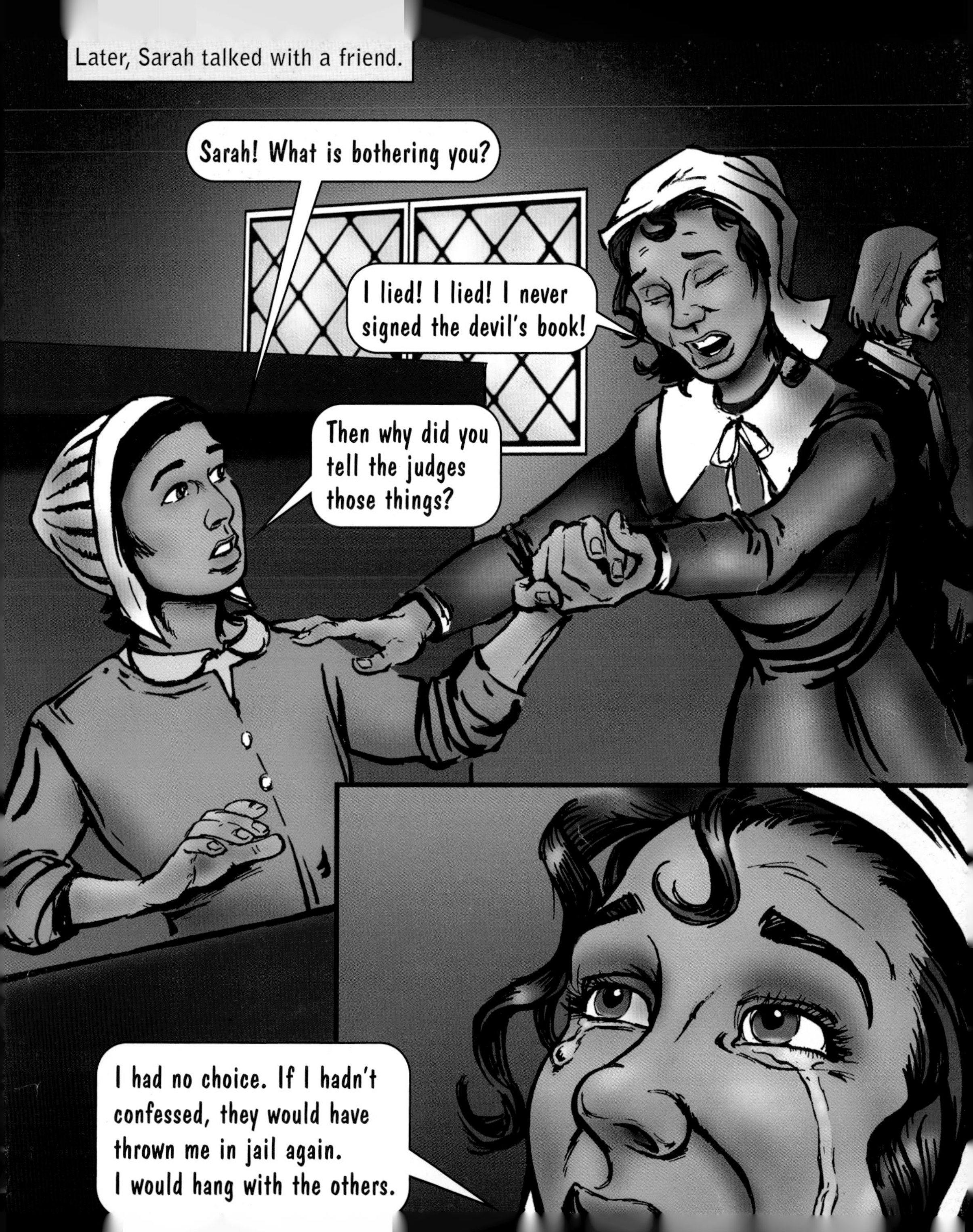
Later, Sarah talked with a friend.
Sarah! What is bothering you?
I lied! I lied! I never signed the devil's book!
Then why did you tell the judges those things?
I had no choice. If I hadn't confessed, they would have thrown me in jail again. I would hang with the others.

CHAPTER · 3

The Trials

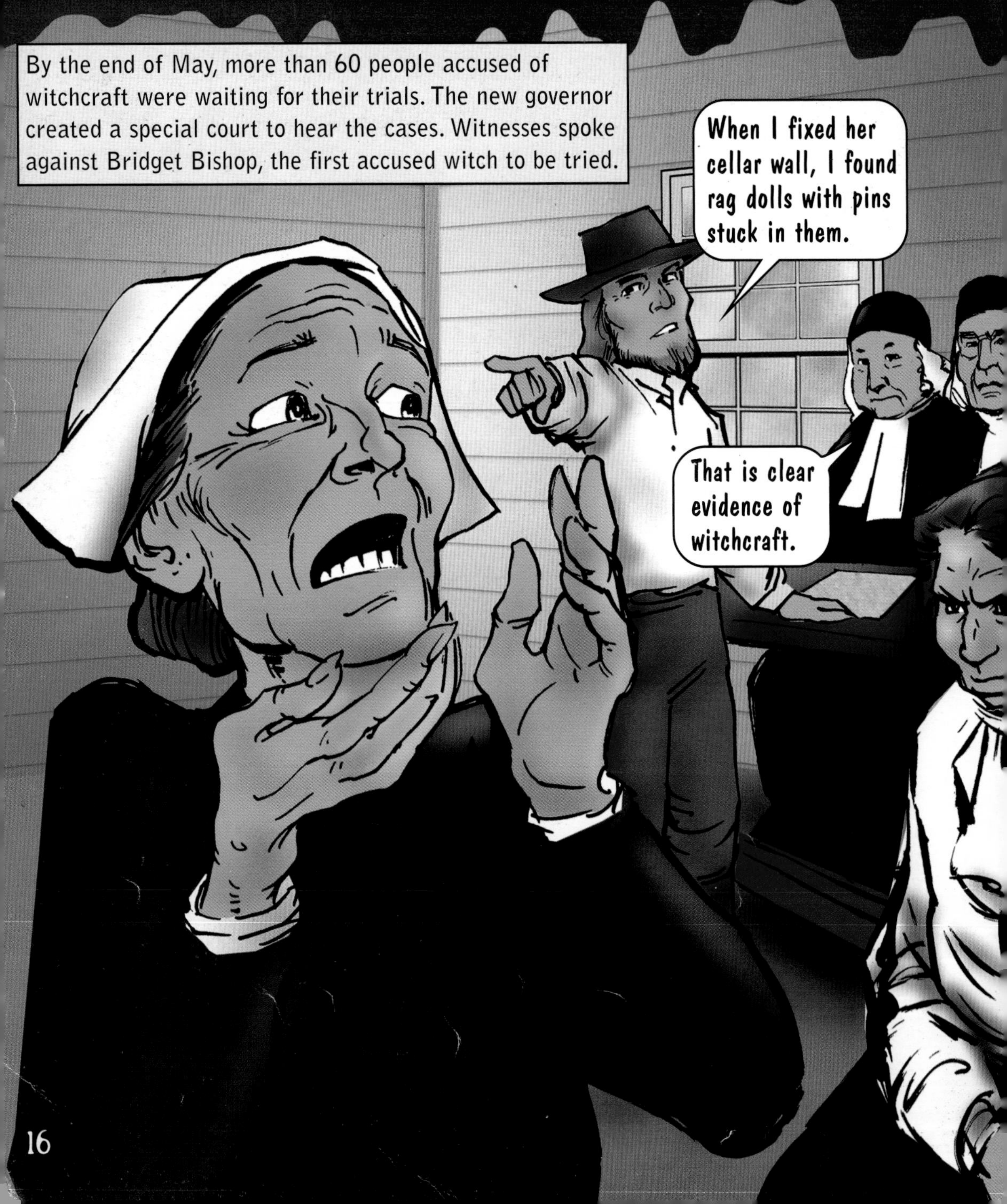
By the end of May, more than 60 people accused of witchcraft were waiting for their trials. The new governor created a special court to hear the cases. Witnesses spoke against Bridget Bishop, the first accused witch to be tried.
When I fixed her cellar wall, I found rag dolls with pins stuck in them.
That is clear evidence of witchcraft.

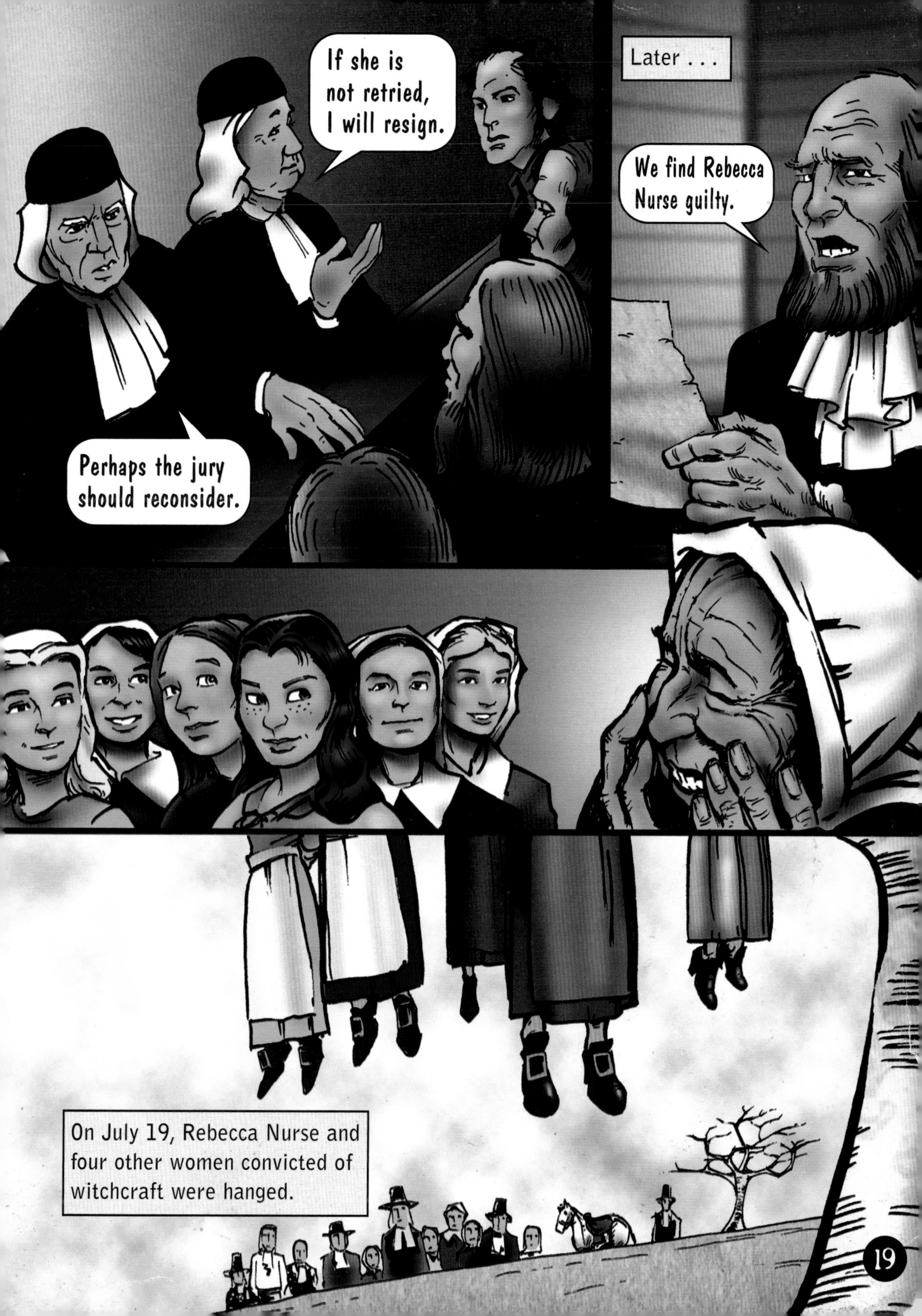
If she is not retried, I will resign.
Perhaps the jury should reconsider.
Later . . .
We find Rebecca Nurse guilty.
On July 19, Rebecca Nurse and four other women convicted of witchcraft were hanged.

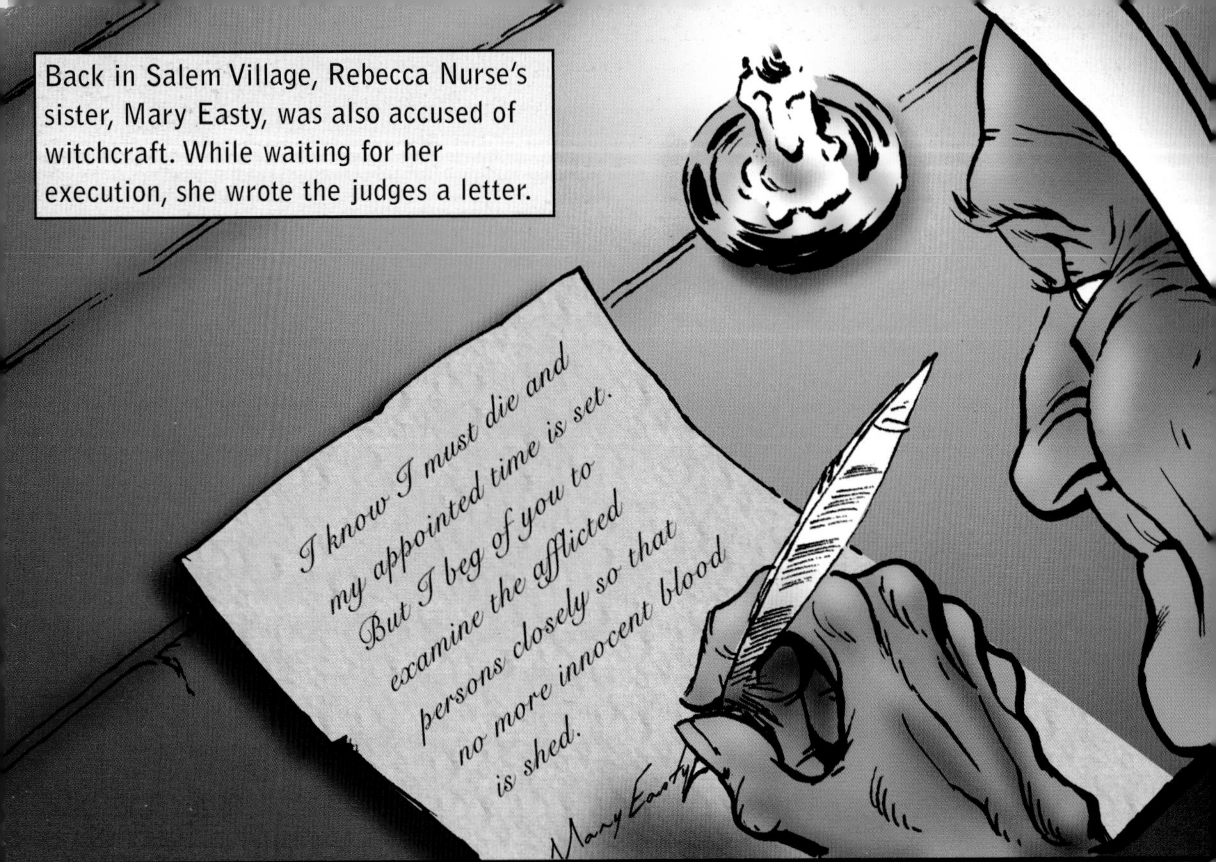
Back in Salem Village, Rebecca Nurse's sister, Mary Easty, was also accused of witchcraft. While waiting for her execution, she wrote the judges a letter.
I know I must die and my appointed time is set. But I beg of you to examine the afflicted persons closely so that no more innocent blood is shed.
Mary Easty

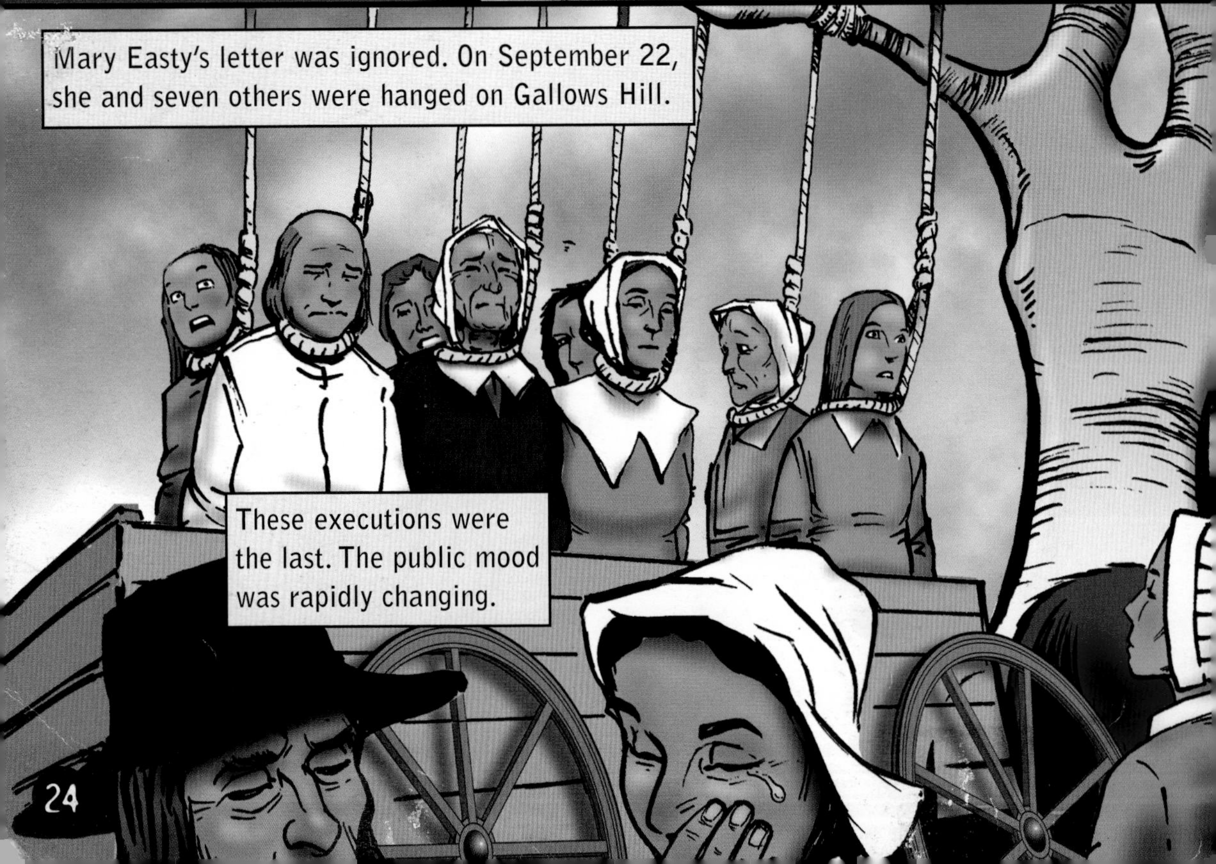
Mary Easty's letter was ignored. On September 22, she and seven others were hanged on Gallows Hill.
These executions were the last. The public mood was rapidly changing.

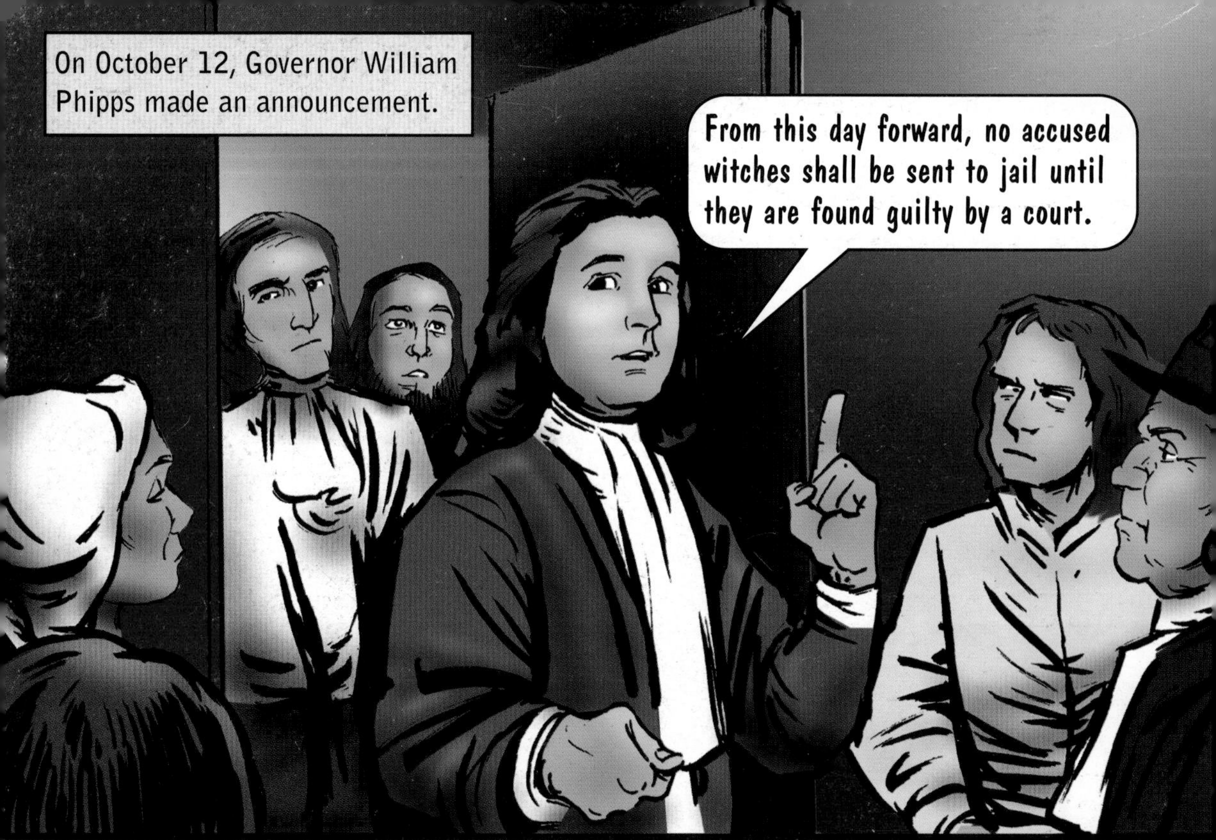
On October 12, Governor William Phipps made an announcement.
From this day forward, no accused witches shall be sent to jail until they are found guilty by a court.

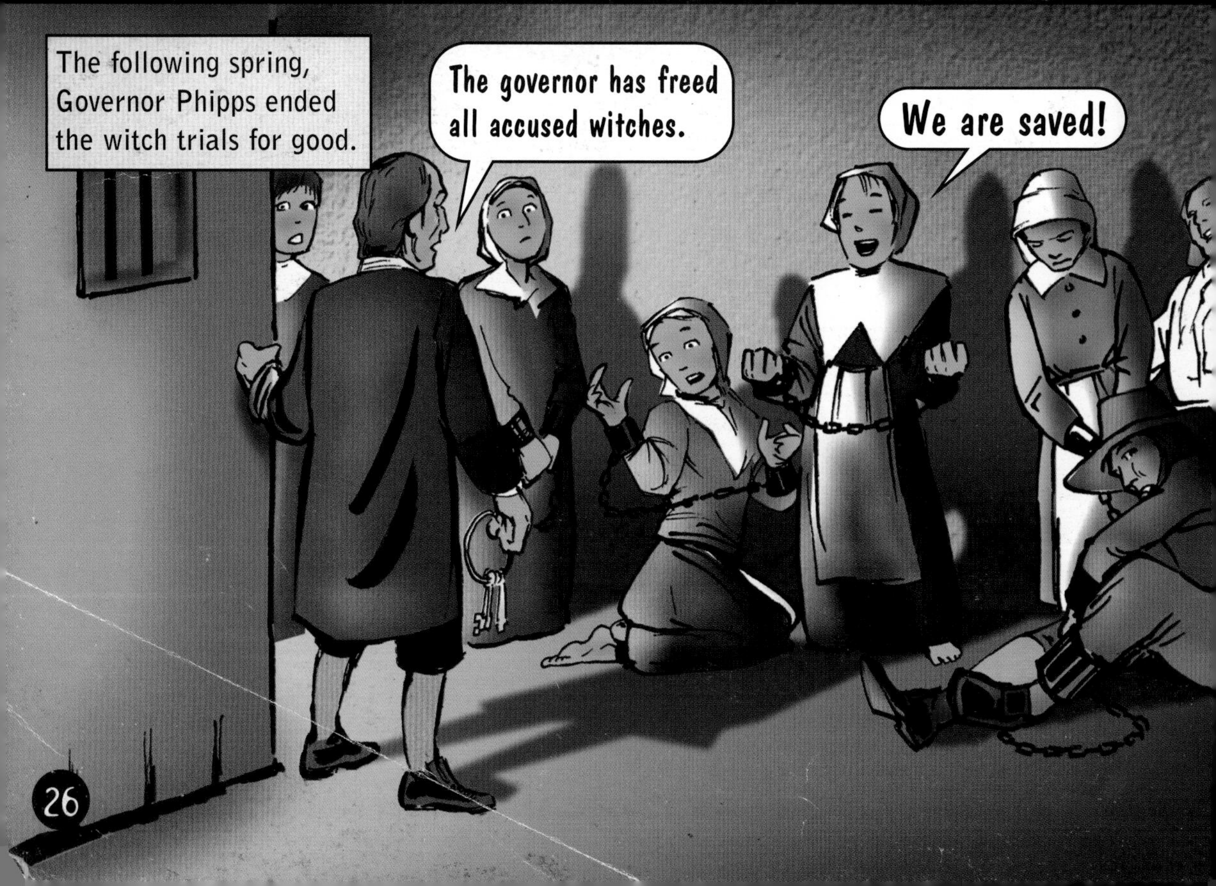
The following spring, Governor Phipps ended the witch trials for good.
The governor has freed all accused witches.
We are saved!

The Salem Witch Trials

✳ Salem Witch Trials Statistics

Number of accusers:	19
Number of people arrested as witches:	about 150
Number of arrested people convicted:	28
Number of convicted people hanged:	19
Other deaths:	4 died in jail
	1 man pressed to death

✳ Dates of Hangings

June 10, 1692	Bridget Bishop
July 19, 1692	Sarah Good, Elizabeth Howe, Susannah Martin, Rebecca Nurse, and Sarah Wilds
August 19, 1692	Reverend George Burroughs, Martha Carrier, George Jacobs, John Proctor, and John Willard
September 22, 1692	Martha Corey, Mary Easty, Alice Parker, Mary Parker, Ann Pudeator, Wilmot Redd, Margaret Scott, and Samuel Wardwell

The Theories

For more than 300 years, historians have tried to explain what caused the witchcraft outbreak in Salem in 1692.

✳ Writing shortly after the trials, Robert Calef thought the accusers were faking their acts. He blamed ministers like Cotton Mather for creating a climate of mass hysteria.

✳ Historians Paul Boyer and Stephen Nissenbaum believe that power struggles and family feuds made people accuse others of witchcraft.

✳ Laurie Winn Carlson, a historian, believed that a disease called encephalitis caused the girls' fits. The disease, spread by mosquitoes, can cause fever, confusion, and seizures.

✳ Chadwick Hansen thought that some people in Salem really did practice witchcraft, and people were very afraid of it.

✳ Bernard Rosenthal offered several reasons that the stories of witchcraft were made up. His reasons included jealousy, getting rid of personal enemies, and people truly believing in witches.

✳ A recent historian, Mary Beth Norton, blamed the climate of fear on wars with American Indians. When the wars began going badly, fearful New Englanders searching for a reason blamed witchcraft.

Glossary

afflicted (uh-FLIK-ted)—being affected by a disease or condition, such as witchcraft

execution (ek-suh-KYOO-shuhn)—the act of putting someone to death as punishment for a crime

hearing (HIHR-ing)—a meeting held by judges to see if there is enough evidence to hold a trial

Lord's Prayer (LORDZ PRAY-ur)—a prayer said by Christians; this prayer appears in the Bible.

mass hysteria (MASS hiss-TEHR-ee-uh)—overwhelming fear or panic felt by many people at one time

Puritans (PYOOR-uh-tuhns)—a group of Protestants in England during the 1500s and 1600s who wanted simple church services and enforced a strict moral code; many Puritans fled England and settled in North America.

Internet Sites

FactHound offers a safe, fun way to find Internet sites related to this book. All of the sites on FactHound have been researched by our staff.

Here's how:

1. Visit *www.facthound.com*
2. Type in this special code **0736838473** for age-appropriate sites. Or enter a search word related to this book for a more general search.
3. Click on the **Fetch It** button.

FactHound will fetch the best sites for you!

Read More

Aronson, Marc. *Witch-hunt: Mysteries of the Salem Witch Trials.* New York: Atheneum Books for Young Readers, 2003.

Boraas, Tracey. *The Salem Witch Trials.* Let Freedom Ring. Mankato, Minn.: Capstone Press, 2004.

Lutz, Norma Jean. *Cotton Mather.* Colonial Leaders. Philadelphia: Chelsea House, 2000.

Somervill, Barbara. *The Massachusetts Colony.* Our Thirteen Colonies. Chanhassen, Minn.: Child's World, 2004.

Bibliography

Boyer, Paul, and Stephen Nissenbaum, eds. *The Salem Witchcraft Papers: Verbatim Transcripts of the Legal Documents of the Salem Witchcraft Outbreak of 1692.* University of Virginia Library, 2003. http://etext.virginia.edu/salem/witchcraft/texts/transcripts.html.

Hill, Frances. *A Delusion of Satan: The Full Story of the Salem Witch Trials.* New York: Doubleday, 1995.

Mather, Cotton. *Memorable Providences Relating to Witchcraft and Possession.* Edinburgh, 1697.

Norton, Mary Beth. *In the Devil's Snare: The Salem Witchcraft Crisis of 1692.* New York: Alfred A. Knopf, 2002.

Starkey, Marion Lena. *The Devil in Massachusetts: A Modern Inquiry into the Salem Witch Trials.* New York: Alfred A. Knopf, 1949. Reprinted with introduction by Aldous Huxley. Alexandria, Va.: Time-Life Books, 1982.

Index